THE PORTAGE POETRY SERIES

SERIES TITLES

Dear Lo
Brady Bove

Sadness of the Apex Predator
Dion O'Reilly

Do Not Feed the Animal
Hikari Miya

The Watching Sky
Judy Brackett Crowe

Let It Be Told in a Single Breath
Russell Thorburn

The Blue Divide
Linda Nemec Foster

Lake, River, Mountain
Mark B. Hamilton

Talking Diamonds
Linda Nemec Foster

Poetic People Power
Tara Bracco (ed.)

The Green Vault Heist
David Salner

There is a Corner of Someplace Else
Camden Michael Jones

Everything Waits
Jonathan Graham

We Are Reckless
Christy Prahl

Always a Body
Molly Fuller

Bowed As If Laden With Snow
Megan Wildhood

Silent Letter
Gail Hanlon

New Wilderness
Jenifer DeBellis

Fulgurite
Catherine Kyle

The Body Is Burden and Delight
Sharon White

Bone Country
Linda Nemec Foster

Not Just the Fire
R.B. Simon

Monarch
Heather Bourbeau

The Walk to Cefalù
Lynne Viti

The Found Object Imagines a Life: New and Selected Poems
Mary Catherine Harper

Naming the Ghost
Emily Hockaday

Mourning
Dokubo Melford Goodhead

Messengers of the Gods: New and Selected Poems
Kathryn Gahl

After the 8-Ball
Colleen Alles

Careful Cartography
Devon Bohm

Broken On the Wheel
Barbara Costas-Biggs

Sparks and Disperses
Cathleen Cohen

Holding My Selves Together: New and Selected Poems
Margaret Rozga

Lost and Found Departments
Heather Dubrow

Marginal Notes
Alfonso Brezmes

The Almost-Children
Cassondra Windwalker

Meditations of a Beast
Kristine Ong Muslim

Cal Freeman's *The Weather of Our Names* is filled with Midwestern existentialism. "People move and of course the mounds of snow / drift and the plows drive like nobody exists. / When the streets are revealed, they're irrevocably changed, cratered like the moon or the bottom of a sea." If as a reader you are too sensitive to the snow, those dense fallings that edge the buildings and line then wet the coats and slush the roads, you could overlook the heartfelt and lyrical family saga or the slow and persistent grieving, the speaker's ambivalent yet helpless moves toward it and the unknown. This collection is attuned to the possibilities of poetry's power to create myth of and provide clarity for one's life. In poems where "snowfall" is ultimately a multi-tonal invention of the speaker, there seems to be a bit of fear of what waits on the other side of the snow's clearing. He admits, "we become / what we cannot look / forward to, the way / a gastropod coils around / itself what is and is not / itself only to be plucked / through its aperture like light." These are admirable conflicts, a reminder that what's inevitable comes whether we look toward it or elsewhere.

—DUSTIN PEARSON
author of *A Season in Hell With Rimbaud*

The world can be a narrow, isolated place, if it weren't for words. And words that are large on the page. And words that are Cal Freeman's. As for this brief foray into Freeman territory, I feel so inadequate to say more about his eclectic and sorrowful and joyful epistles and fungibles. This is a book to leave bedside, drink that before-bed whiskey earlier than later, and return to this very Detroit Dearborn Dublin tome.

—RUSSELL THORBURN
author of *Let It Be Told in a Single Breath*

The Weather
of Our Names

poems

Cal Freeman

CORNERSTONE PRESS
UNIVERSITY OF WISCONSIN-STEVENS POINT

Cornerstone Press, Stevens Point, Wisconsin 54481
Copyright © 2025 John Freeman
www.uwsp.edu/cornerstone

Printed in the United States of America.

Library of Congress Control Number: 2025941890
ISBN: 978-1-960329-98-1

Cornerstone Press titles are produced in courses and internships offered by the Department of English at the University of Wisconsin–Stevens Point.

DIRECTOR & PUBLISHER
Dr. Ross K. Tangedal

EXECUTIVE EDITORS
Jeff Snowbarger, Freesia McKee

EDITORIAL DIRECTOR
Brett Hill

SENIOR EDITORS
Paige Biever, Eva Nielsen, Reilly Crous

PRESS STAFF
Lilly Kulbeck, Abby Paulsen, Brianna Loving, Sophie McPherson, Sam Bjork, Madison Schultz, Autumn Vine, Allison Lange

ALSO BY CAL FREEMAN:

POEMS

I.

II.

III.

I.

Thought on Thought With Fried Chicken Getting Cold

My mother stands in the common area of Applegate
Nursing Home reciting Eugene Field
to a cohort of closed-head injury residents.
She coaches Anna Babich, who twenty years ago
was tossed from the back of her boyfriend's
Harley when a truck sideswiped them
on Telegraph Road one summer night.
Anna blurts out a couple words
before her tongue contorts into a tangle
of fricatives and spit. "The gingham dog,"
she says. *And the calico cat*, my mother prompts
her to continue. "Side by side" *on the table sat.*
And so my mother spends her lunch hour
while my father and I sit and listen
and the Kentucky Fried Chicken
we brought gets cold. But there is news
to be gathered from the Dutch clock
and the Chinese plate, from the bovine eyes
of Anna Babich, Joe Palmatier, and Ellen Wright
as they learn a stray line or two of bad verse
from a pale woman in a squat brick building
that might once have been the site of an orchard
gate opening onto rows of apple trees.
In retrogenesis, we end up as children
swinging on that gate and plucking apples
from the ancient hybrid trees grafted
into something we can wrap our limbs around,
losing all but the most distant memories.
We can't agree on what is meant by "mind,"
but perhaps it is a ragged book
of schoolroom verse, a small carton
of fast food, grease congealing, a stone tower
near the railyards of Woodhaven, Michigan
flashing red and white lights while scrambling
freight along the twisting tracks.

Dichotomy Paradox as a Non-Fungible Token

I want a different year in clean, white snow.
I want the rapid senescence afforded the possum
before trauma. Just before that moment of collapse.
It's not for play. It's so it can't remember what befalls it.
A possum isn't playing possum. I want my father back.
I want a different father with the same tastes
and the same loves. I want a different flower
than what blooms in the boxwood hedges
without germination. I want to read the book
Melville's Final Voyage which my father owns in a dream.
I'm not a seafarer, but I'm not faring well,
I want to say. The snow that fell as heavy slush
early in the day has turned to eider down.
People move and of course the mounds of snow
drift and the plows drive like nobody exists.
When the streets are revealed, they're irrevocably changed,
cratered like the moon or the bottom of a sea.
A neighbor offered me her snow blower,
but I prefer shovel marks knife-edge to the driveway.
It's hard to imagine what the phrase "coming back"
must've meant once. To have it mean anything
one would have to watch the plow returning
and not have picked up the trajectory of the turn
before the vehicle began coming back.
One would have to want to have a different life
in clear, white snow and want a different bloom
than the one created by the snow that February day,
along the boxwood hedgerows with wine
in the decanter and thought-heavy thoughts
for the ones who left us in the garden. My voice hissing
through clenched teeth. I want a different echo
than the possum. I want a different name.

For as long as I can remember
I've been both annoyed and haunted by my name.
I don't think this is a unique relationship
to have to one's name. I imagine everyone
is at times annoyed and at other times haunted
by their names, but I dwell on mine far too much.
Others are even brave enough to change them,
and I'm not talking about some monosyllabic nom de plume
haphazardly applied, but legally change them.
My name is why it takes me so long to clear the car,
to broom it off before starting it and scraping the windows.
These are too many names and numerals for one life,
but they're so indelibly correct that I hum them
in the cold snow and again in the warm car.
It's what I don't know back there at the root
and am too listless to learn that does the haunting.
It's who I don't know. It's the theology of Jean Cauvin
and how he came to be known as John Calvin.
The prevenient grace some of them have been afforded.
I give up a little more every day. I drive to Bar 342
for corned beef sliders. I read Fanny Howe's *Second Childhood*
as I sip Canadian Club whiskey and wait for my lunch.
The man next to me has a voice like a half-empty matchbox
rattling itself awake. He doesn't know how
he's doing yet. He's here to retrieve a car
left in the parking lot. He asks if the Howe
is my AA booklet. *John John John, and John* I read
in "Between Delays." I underline the four instances
of my name with a keno pencil.
John is his name too, I find out, and his voice
isn't like a matchbox I decide, as I note the slack skin
around his throat, it's more like an accidental whisper,
a light breeze over dying wheat. I tell him I'd have flunked out
within a few hours, but I've got step one down
(I don't think you can actually flunk out of their program).

I read a poem called "Loneliness," scarf down my sliders,
and pay my tab. There's too much data in this place—
keno screens, an internet jukebox, a baby shower
with a chicken wing buffet. There's too much data
in the enjambed lines of the book, what a friend of mine
has called "hangnail stanzas," for me to latch onto
anything other than my name and this personification
of loneliness that might engage such a name in actions
like clearing snow and driving to lunch.
John follows me out. A green balloon is trapped
in the door handle. He warns me not to pop it.
He paraphrases the Book of John as he lights a cigarette,
says the truth will set me free. John's my name, he explains,
and that's from the Book of John and I should try to live
my life by the idea that the truth will set you free.
I thank him. I don't tell him how homonyms ensnare us
or how the sunlight on ragged snow renders the romance
of hunkering down remote. It's too easy to drive now.
For anyone to truly come back the road would have to adopt
a chronology of hours. I don't want the road to adopt
a chronology of hours. I could be going out
for all they know. They who paved this road with too many miles.
The more of it they plow, the less of me spins out.
There's an elegance to Zeno's paradox that circumvents
the civic mind and a loveliness to leftover weather
that one mustn't lose in the sun.
I need to have my tires rotated, something. A good barroom needs
good haruspices the way prophecy needs a self to fulfill
its self-fulfilling augurs. They don't have to do much
but observe the damage and guess right.
I'll heat my liver for a reading any afternoon.

The City of Champions

Every purchase is a slovenly humiliation,
yet the new historicist in me
wants to tell you what I bought
at the Sunoco station at the corner
of Butler and Holmes in Pittsburgh, Pennsylvania
circa some year of our lord—a three-pack
of Trojan Ecstasy condoms
and an eight-pack of Tums antacid tablets.
I also wanted to buy a banana
but feared looking ludicrous at checkout.
Another part of me, the part of me
that drank wine while wandering
the Allegheny Cemetery that afternoon,
doesn't want to share my consumer habits
with anyone. Wingbeats, an incline
up the staggered stone steps calving
from the hillock, gravity is different here.
The upper half of you levitates toward pinnacles
while everything below the sacrum
feels heavy. The anniversary
of the immaculate reception is nigh,
the first since Franco Harris's death.
Throughout Pittsburgh, on roads
that veer into chasmic river gorges,
they are planning an ungodly celebration
of grace through happenstance.

Adrian Dantley (AD) Circa 1890s

The night Larry Bird famously stole Isiah Thomas's inbound pass
I was with my mother at Circa 1890s Saloon
across Cass Avenue from Wayne State University
where my father was teaching *The Tempest*
to a group of bored undergrads in State Hall.
It was 1987, or circa 1890s if one takes the long view of history.
AD was my favorite Pistons player that year.
My mother was bantering with a drunk Boston fan
who, as she put it, "was looking to get his teeth knocked out
rooting for Boston in a Cass Corridor bar."
My father let his class out early to catch the end of the game.
We had them down one with three seconds to go
and possession of the ball. It looked like
we were coming back to Detroit with a 3-2 series lead
and were finally going to vanquish the Celtics.
"Larry Bird sucks eggs on Saturday nights,"
my mother taunted the guy. It was Tuesday.
My parents shared an '85 Ford Escort back then,
and we picked my father up from work
Tuesday nights so he didn't have to ride
the Warren Avenue bus after dark.
My father laughed at my mother's trash talking
as he sipped his Newcastle Ale. Gone now
circa 2020 is Circa 1890s, its façade of curved
white pillars that never blocked the rain
and faded to the color of cigarette ash
as the paint leached and decades passed,
known as "the teeth" to Wayne State students, gone.
All bars circa 1890s get loud with animated talk
about little matters that matter little alone
but creep up in aggregate at the end of a stanza.
Basketball is a series of meticulous little matters.

AD and Bill Laimbeer setting brutal, off-the-ball
screens out of bounds. Barroom histrionics
around cathode ray tube televisions, full fathom five
into which the ghost of Boston Garden stowed
our hopes (in the deciding game seven AD
would knock himself unconscious diving
for a loose ball). Wondrous and strange,
my mother's invective, the beer foam in my father's beard,
Larry Bird stepping before that fated pass
like an interference beam (the holomovement
that holds them there in their spectral dimensions),
his quick toss to Dennis Johnson for a lay-up
with a second left. AD dropped 25 in game five.
His right leg was two inches shorter than his left,
but he had a such a quick first step (Kevin McHale
was a wicket jammed in wet cement
when he tried to guard him) and a deadly flat-footed shot.
Isiah never liked him, though, and Dennis Rodman
got too many minutes for his taste. When they traded AD in 1989,
I sobbed on my mother's shoulder in our living room
(yellow light on rough-hewn mahogany paneling,
all that never happens in the interior of a place
happens to us, directly, there. The secret
mind of a university swimming in imported tap beer
and popcorn, free popcorn. Circa 1890s,
a joke that was easy to miss but would define
an epoch in a public university's life)
like we were saying goodbye forever to somebody
we loved. It's the first time I remember feeling that way.

Racing Simulcast as a Non-Fungible Token

"The body" is so physiologically vague
I begin to think my experiences are not my own,
but the femurs, ligaments,
and muscles still hoist their frame.

I stand up, at times, in other words.
In the evenings I walk down to the creek
to count the barn swallows and watch
the empty tennis court.

Ivan Ilyich was mystified by a nagging pain
in his side. It's possible to laugh it off
as a foppish accident incurred
while hanging drapes. Better.

But there's more to less than that.
The Scotch tape beneath the roof shingles
hisses in the draft from the air conditioning unit.
Winter clippers and piss-warm summer

convections can't tear it away.
The other afternoon, I was in Soaring Eagle
Casino watching the racing simulcast
from Finger Lakes Downs,

hoping to spot Andrew who's sweating
thoroughbreds now, Andrew,
whom my mother considered my best friend.
What he hoped to be I can't know.

Doing what you love can cause as much damage
as the next shambolic gift—
purse race, fillies;
colt claiming round, six furlongs;

maiden claiming; driveway stones,
abiota—heat, rainfall, mud etc.—
Queen of Cups. They have these teeth
they click at anyone.

I fear the indiscretion, not the beast.
I'm not a student of precision.
I don't stand
at balustrades of rain to listen.

A Brief Survey of Regional Consumer Markets

By "doge" I mean Lord of a city state
and not the fallen coin. By "fallen"
I mean devaluation of a cryptocurrency
and not a penny tumbling through
the stale waters of a museum fountain
in the mind of someone's wish.
Problem being, things called each other
without meaning each other. Problem being
sometimes, the preposterous is true.

A convenience store on the outskirts
of a campground reopens near midnight,
and my mother buys popcorn.
We are staying in a Winnebago owned
by Uncle Emmett, a scrap metal magnate.
A movie plays on a portable 12"TV.
It's the early days of VHS. The disposable
tin pan domes over a propane flame.

Three decades later I'm in Ocean Beach
in a neighborhood full of crows
and feral parrots. The atavistic hippie
culture here has figured out the languorous
truth that to free a flock of parrots makes
a provenance of their proliferation.
A terribly intrusive chatter culminates
in horror and enchantment.
You wanna buy some weed
from a beach bum in need?
No, but there's good mezcal in this town.
The birds go on in dactyls on tiled roofs
and sickly palms. I wouldn't call it

a heroic meter in their voices.
Package ships on the horizon
stultify the tongue. Cranes hover
over the bay up in Oakland waiting
to unload them. The containers
are preformed to latch onto freight
cars and freightliner beds. It's ingenuity
of a sort that expedites succor
leaving aside all questions of the good.

Schedule K-1 Form From Southern Pennsylvania
Propane Company as a Non-Fungible Token

My mother's CPA says she needs a K-1 form
from the Southern Pennsylvania Propane Company,
a pass-through entity she's apparently invested in.
He tells me they are tax harvesting her losers.

I don't understand what any of this means,
but it sounds like the language of my father's death,
the kind of language I've been hearing
since my father's death. Bloodless drivel
that keeps everyone arm's length from what's at stake.

I imagine a poem called "Instructions for the Passing Spirit."
I write, *Pass through the provisional entity*
of the body into the southern Allegheny gorges
and lacustrine pools that wane
in the February sun. Harvest what is reticent
to yield, harvest the organs that were treated
gently during his life (she told you
at the time of his death that your father
had given the gift of life).

It was impossible to get over there last week
in the freezing rain. The trees were cut-glass candelabras,
diaphanous
in their ice. There was a precarity in their beauty.
We knew the limbs could break and knock
the power out or worse. Our world
was so conductive then, stray voltage everywhere.

But today the afternoon unspools without effect,
like the macadam along the flat road

to her house. The dumbest dog
my parents ever owned, the last dog they
owned together was euthanized last month.
My mother seemed unfazed. I listen
for its signature racket as I walk up
to the crumbling stoop, folded quire of papers
in my left hand, the waspy soffits
pissing down the run-off ice. I recall
something good from last December,
pan-fried pickerel on Willow china,
dry German Riesling in Waterford flutes,
my mother reciting Alfred Noyes
and Robert Frost while drinking wine.

Walleye Carcass as a Non-Fungible Token

I'm not here to tell you what rejuvenates,
but I know—a walk out to the pier
at Pointe Mouillee, a conversation

about sonations of swans,
parentheses and vocatives,
little lives along the way.

Your liver has regenerated
countless times over
and the blanched and frozen skull

is of an indeterminate animal
whose only thoughts centered
on lapping water mites

and unscrupulous predation.
It's easy to kick
at the profundity of blunder,

to turn over spiky rows
of unpinioned teeth,
but have you ever loved yourself enough

to posit a desire?
It's a fish, not a bird.
The best spirits don't leave

their corpses to watch you sleep,
yet you seem unconcerned
with the wandering of the worst ones.

The terns slash occultations
in the fog before the barrier isle.
The pilot house of the freighter

seems to levitate without a hull.
The joints groan like bulwarks.
In the Lydian modality of the wind,

there is a desire to interrogate
the offal. I've got less than one octave.
I look back at her just once.

Canada, Approximately

Uncle Viktor owned a bar in Rockwood called the Tegmine, after a crab-shaped group of stars in the constellation Cancer, but there's far less to steer by if you're headed toward Ontario or Monroe in a speedboat, sailboat, or cabin cruiser. I told Uncle Viktor, *If you're heading toward Put-In-Bay in your cabin cruiser, you can't be counting on the stars; you should have more than stars to go on.* I made a joke about the lump crab sandwich, his signature Zeta Cancri, and Rockwood bologna when I sat in the Tegmine one afternoon and drank. *I'll give you the river,* I said, as if it were mine, but Uncle Viktor knew the river like he knew the swollen veins on the backs of his hands. The Huron full of PFAS, gobies, and damsel flies rippling the blue-green algae. Uncle Viktor would stop his bicycle to eat a lump crab sandwich and watch the freighters plod toward the smaller islands of Ontario. Perhaps it wasn't worth it to keep the beer in the cooler and the heat in the ducts and the former owner's ghost upstairs, or to keep the taciturn old man who set out our cold longnecks in his employ behind the plank all those decades. The Tegmine won't be there when we re-emerge. The Boblo Island Amusement Park, where Uncle Viktor would drive us in those emphysemic knock-off Model Ts, has been gone for decades too. *Believe me when I tell you the boundary waters belie all consequence,* he said once. *I have a friend a few short nautical miles from here who remembers me as a bight before a copse of trees obscuring riverbanks through the lenses of a pair of Nikon Aculons. We don't see more precisely with binoculars or any of the Tuscan's instruments; we don't know our noses from a nation or a bar rail from a floe of river ice,* he added. It's the kind of vestigial talk that keeps a gone place alive while the bills and notices pile up. They could take the Tegmine, but he knows that group of stars like he knows his breadth of boundary waters, like he knows who hauls on waders to go haunting in our debts.

Fandango Hall Matchbook
as a Non-Fungible Token

Manila timecard in the slot to stamp
the hour and minute it ostensibly began—

that kitchen where Nancy dangled a cigarette
in her lips above a vat of soup,

a precarious simmer. The Fandango Hall
matchbook advertised smoke-eaters,

signature fried chicken, plenty of well light [sic]
parking, and a festive atmosphere that kept

the Iron Mustangs Motorcycle Club
coming back for their annual party.

It's impossible to explain how gratifying it was
to show up first the morning after

cabarets and gather blunt roaches
from tin ashtrays on the tables,

to unroll them and pour the shake
into a Ziploc bag from which you'd smoke

for days. You might return then
to your Buick Century in the parking lot

and listen to "Pigs on the Wing"
or Jim Carroll reading from "The Narrows"

while waiting for Gil Garza, Ben Brown,
Jonathan Chapel, the Jenner Brothers. Knowing the day

would be stretched out the way dawn
gets stretched in a blear of exhaust fumes,

you'd have wasted every lovely sentiment
that rattled in your head by nine.

Seagulls would linger there
to scavenge chicken bones, butts, wet napkins

smeared with grease. They exercised
such indiscriminate hungers. What would you be

setting up for in that empty hall? Retirement,
nuptials, some other rite with a puzzling diagram

of oval tables? One morning you retrieved
the numbered ping pong balls from the riser

and laughed about the plastic trolls, those amulets
the old women had forgotten at Bingo

the night before, their neon hair standing
against the wicked fates.

Annotations While Waiting for the Mail and Thinking of My Mother

Once I found my mother trembling before the computer screen, unable to speak.

If assembling one poem out of several unsuccessful openings constitutes a day's work...

If it wouldn't be more worthwhile to trim the boxwood hedges out back...

Someone was always coming for her, each moment the penultimate one before arrest.

Images garnered from old films, psychiatric hospitals with neo-Tudor embrasures, handcuffs, white jackets, soft-soled tennis shoes squeaking on asbestos tile...

(the latest acquisitions: *deodand, flensed, massif, skirl, scute, vesicle*)

[reading Forrest Gander]

If the limits of my language...

If the film *One Flew Over the Cuckoo's Nest* informed my mother's psychosis...

If you can keep your head... she would often recite from memory.

If the world itself is the great contingency against which psychosis is measured...

If the visual language of paranoia achieves verisimilitude...

White jackets, handcuffs, squeaking soft-soled shoes on asbestos tile…

If the elliptical orbits into oblivion and back…

If the elliptical is truly asymptotic…

If its function is to create a metalanguage out of tautology and error…

If the entire field culminates in the Epicurean delight of being told what we believe we know…

(*aporia, atomic fact, proposition, substance*)

If "anyone can either be the case or not be the case, and everything else remain the same…"

[reading *Tractatus*]

If the mind is a deodand confiscated by the institution

for acting as the agent of its own laborious death…

If the subject has been adequately flensed…

If your head is in a vise do not presume to lecture

my mother about the disposal of un-swallowed pills

or the harmlessness of the Schwan's Dairy delivery truck

that has left surveillance equipment with a neighbor //

with a neighbor across the road. If the snow outside

is diffuse powder impossible to pack…

Derecho

What does it mean that you lived on Shenandoah Street,
a name so far removed from its whistling valley?

Near the back of the yard was a concrete slab stained
tobacco-brown by eastern cottonwood leaves.

Those trees grow too quick, top-heavy and weak
in sandy loam, routinely toppling in summer storms.

Once there was a shed there, but it was blown away
by the green storm of 1980. The trace is a great container

for the aorist tense. It's a serrated, toothy leaf.
It's a great leaf shape for tracing and incising what's befallen

Me, and has befallen you before, and thus keeps. Even the tree
is gone. The tree is unsurprisingly gone.

My father saw a Volkswagen fall
from the sky into the parking lot of Amato's Restaurant

on his way home. He and my mother huddled in the stairwell
where there were no windows. I love what it means

for trees felled by storms before your birth to cradle
concrete in their roots. I love the way the bowed

fence post can't go back to how it was but tells us
how it was all the same. You can get forty years

out of a good fence post. I've gotten more than that
out of comparable equipment. I meant to say I'm afraid

of storms and other things as I stagger into middle age.
I meant to find a more precise noun than things, Shenandoah,

whistling valley. I meant to say you can't see the middle
from where you're at, to explain my use of second-person

sooner, how its reverse bow echo is meant to foretell
a straight line wind. How *I meant to say* has less to do

with botched intentions than the mystery of utterance itself.
How I hope we don't become what we haven't said.

Below the Renaissance Towers

I hate the river walk—the fishers
fumbling largemouths silvered
like clean windows

of the icon's eastern face
before tossing them to disappear
into the murk, girth-sore

and cankered, changed.
I'm not eating this lunch,
not sharing pastrami with flies.

Glug and plash
of currents in the strait,
gnawing contemplation

when it comes time for some
fisher of men to toss me back,
for the deeds to be occluded

by the brackish shadows—
it wasn't yet my turn in the hyaline
terror of the Coleman cooler.

What is it about water
that begs encomiums for birds?
The sub-categories of heron

(I could've simply stayed home),
symbols of patience (egret,
great blue) proliferate

and get mixed up with languor
when anyone can
step out the door and start

walking, unintentionally
proclaiming the beauty
in the lyric's slow accretions—

unhooked and fed between
the barbicans to water.

Starting Gate

In a field of Canadian thistle and clover,
bald in patches with sand,
in the burial place for all the Pembrokes' horses,
a blue starting gate is anchored to the earth
by knotted Virginia creeper strands
as if, like those moving starting gates
on the backs of Cadillacs at harness races,
it might float away. If a horse walks through
a starting gate's chute, it will load
into a trailer, the logic goes,
which is why the old man bought this one
and hauled it here three decades ago.
But if we extrapolate too much
from a situation, we lose sight
of the horseness of horses.
Of course, of course, it's not
that the tautology's shambolic.
Instead, it's affirming to those
who already know. Andrew trots bareback
on a white speckled mare named Silest,
her sides fat from having foaled three months before.
There was a time he was a trusted friend.
I don't talk to him anymore.
The blue paint has leached from the gate,
and nobody's serious about horse shows
or harness racing. In a field of Canadian thistle
and clover, the bones of buried horses
wait to be enraptured. When Silest died,
they placed her on a muddy tarp
and dragged her back here while bluebottles
suckled at her girth sores. I don't think we cried.
I'd remember Silest years later

when my mother lay on a sleeping bag
on our basement floor surrounded
by family pictures, including a black-and-white
boyhood photo of my father riding
a Shetland pony in Tulsa, OK.
My mother's skin sallow as the sawdust streaks
in Silest's coat, her half-closed eyelids quivering
as though scattering summer flies.

Ode to Coca-Cola, Helium, Carbon

A half-drunk bottle of Coca-Cola
rests on Johnny McGlynn's tombstone.
A couple of helium balloons are tied to it too.
Sarah wonders what the story is.
Neither of us knew Johnny McGlynn,
brand-loyal McGlynn, lover of soda pop
McGlynn. He's neighbors
with my father now. My father's his new neighbor.
Sarah left wire flowers in the brass stand
next to my father's name on the black
columbarium wall across the little road
from McGlynn's tombstone.
My mother, Peggy O'Neill, picked this spot,
called "companionship grove,"
for its proximity to the river.
Johnny McGlynn's Coca-Cola bottle
puts me in mind of that famous jar
in Tennessee, the way it bends
the Huron River and Huron River
Drive to the cemetery's will.
Hot Coca-Cola is disgusting
to consider on this muggy day.
It's supposed to storm later.
My mother worries about the flowers
in the rain and wind. I recite
"The Beautiful American Word,
Sure" by Delmore Schwartz
to the black marble box, but the town
of Flat Rock is stone-deaf to poetry.
You can't get the words to make music.
I'm not finishing poems much these days.
I keep name-checking my father's

favorite poets, though, instead
of saying what I don't know how to say
about finitude and grief. Death is heavy,
like the tombstone of Johnny McGlynn.
It bends the space around it to accelerate
the light, but grief is more
like the helium balloons that pretend
to lift his grave; they work at it all day,
this futile lifting.
Sarah notes how strange it is to see
my mother's name beneath my father's
even though her death date's unfulfilled—
open paren, closed paren, open paren,
parents, parent. There's so much
I don't want to tell you. There's even more
I don't want to hear myself say, like
I'm equal to the task of leaving
crass symbols with the dead.
The story of Coca-Cola is well-known
and engaging for cocaine's
appearance as a character, but it's nothing
when contrasted with the story of helium,
that yellow spectral line observed
during a solar eclipse in 1868,
first among the earthly noble gases,
second among elements in ubiquity.
Carbon, which mycelium borrows
from tree roots to break down matter,
is fourth in abundance; the carbon cycle's
why there's little left of your neighbor,
Johnny McGlynn, Father.
But they treated you to fire
and put you in a box which I placed
inside the columbarium wall.
I think you'd like hearing *they treated you to fire*

from inside your marble; it reminds me
of Milton's *burning marl.*
I look at the carbonated beverage
flat in Flat Rock and remember how
I placed a box in a vault
and it made phosphorous run to the river,
and algae stopped the running river, Father.
You watch now like a heron from your
gabbled roost. Johnny McGlynn
sucks ice in 4/4 time. My mother
thinks you deserve a swifter river.
This one's gold-green like a pile
of newly minted bills or St. Patrick's Day
swag scattered in a parking lot.
Pretend luck starved of oxygen,
this way we speak of graves
and what you would've liked.

Epistle to the Donut Shop

Dear Warren Avenue, dear aluminum green awning
beneath which people waiting for the Dearborn bus
would dodge the rain: Polish women in dripping babushkas
clutching shopping bags from Fairlane Mall, young Black men
headed for the suburbs to look for work, Lebanese
millwrights going home from a grueling shift at Rouge,
dear Golden Boy Donuts, I write to you as I would write
to my parents if letters were still necessary, and they are,
of course, just as every outmoded medium gives us
so much we do not know we need. Dear father
seated in a booth behind a wall of windows drinking coffee,
reading student essays pulled from an ink-scarred manila folder,
glancing out at the avenue guttering with puddles
and discarded shopping bags while my three-year-old self eats
glazed cake donut holes and listens to Helen and Elizabeth,
immigrant first cousins who owned the place, speak to each other
in Polish (my childhood is narrated by languages
I still don't understand except in cadence and intent,
my mother speaking Spanish with Maria Chavez,
our next door neighbor, for hours while the neighborhood
kids ran in the spume of an uncapped hydrant in July;
Shadia Shamsedean calling her children inside in Arabic
as the street lights buzzed on). I would watch the water runnel
off of you and splay like feathers. Once I tripped in a mud puddle
in the alley, and Helen fished me out and bathed me
in the prep kitchen where they kneaded and cut the dough
and sifted powdered sugar over the Euclidean shapes of pastries,
swaddling me in warm dish towels while we waited
for my clothes to dry. My mother worked midnights in triage
at Receiving Hospital, and she would sleep during the day,
which meant that while we were eating donuts, she was dreaming
of gunshot victims and the stunned doughy faces of cardiac

arrest, of stab wounds like sequined dime purses, near overdoses
with glassy eyes and pustuled forearm scabs, police badges
glinting in halogen light, which meant that while
my father read bad prose written by the 18-year-old
children of auto workers for Composition I at Wayne State
University, my mother's dreams were narrated by a tinny voice
reciting injuries and traumas into an analogue telephone
receiver over a crackling PA. Dear donut shop,
you are gone, not gone exactly, but your lime-green façade
has been painted pink and your smell of dough and coffee
has been replaced by garlic and kibbie, and the family
that owns this place came here fleeing a war the way
Helen and Elizabeth came here fleeing war in a wholly
different world, yet a world defined by those twin forces
of violence and refuge, and I love this place still as I love
my mother and father while remembering donut holes
and steaming Styrofoam cups of coffee. Dear Hamido Restaurant,
dear Golden Boy, dear father, dear mother traumatized by all
that you have seen, dear Dearborn, I eat kafta in the same
building, watching the blacktop avenue blear with rain
and oil, women in hijabs pushing little wire carts out
of Arabic markets, abjad liturgical script above the English
signage, and I'm nostalgic for what hasn't really changed.

Stafford Essentials Corduroy Jacket
as a Non-Fungible Token

The coat can't love you
the way your father did.
It isn't clear how.
Corduroy lined in silk.
Two breast pockets.
Two interior pockets.
Your father hoarded napkins.
This much you can say.
It reveals something.
All your father's annotations
have, to this point,
been disappointing,
his visitations ludic and oneiric.
One note in the margins of
A Midsummer Night's Dream
says, *Be a good inheritor*
of tropes. If I had brothers,
they would've been turned into swans.
It's nearing eighty today,
superfluous coat.
Imaginary hands around the shoulders,
fabric of want.
You can almost picture them,
your father's hands crumpling
paper napkins
and shoving them deep into
a pocket near his heart.

II.

Prologue to a Fiction

The romance of place said both congruous and incongruous events occurred generations apart but seemed overlaid because of where they happened. Said geography meant more to history than time. Said the sod fields of western Wayne County stretched out like a bay at night. Said what we call the soul may not be anything more than tributaries bounding over glacial scars like horses, the broad flats of rivers that pour into basins of ancient lakes, the moraines carved by the violence of compression.

The romance of place said the drive across the Grosse Ile Parkway Bridge, the way the grates of the bridge tugged at the tires of my grandmother's Ford Escort, and how the lights of the steel factory spangled the black surface of the river were evidence that some minor riparian god had blessed us. Had said a prayer for our cars, those status symbols, sad vessels of utility; said a prayer for cars given away and cars restored, cars kept for posterity, cars that cruised in the bliss of perseverant beauty, cars crossing over rivers. The romance of place said you could get nowhere in this region without one. Said we had been crossing back and forth on that grated county bridge since before any of us were born.

The romance of place said a teenager named Whatley flattened his father in the parking lot of a Belleville honky-tonk one autumn night while the father's mistress looked on. Said years ago, when my own father was in graduate school and writing his dissertation about Thomas More's *Utopia*, he drove his car to Belleville and attended a church service. The romance of place said the homily and the saintly prose swimming around in his head made him fill up with the fervor of a saint and donate the little Honda to a country pastor. It wasn't much of a car to speak of, a two-door Civic with rust spots in the floor, but it was certainly more than my parents had to give. The romance of place said the next day when my dad seemed to have forgotten where he had been or where he had left the car, my mother borrowed my grandmother's car to drive out there and offer an awkward explanation about my father internalizing the lives of Catholic saints and explain how this giving was really manic behavior driven by extreme duress. She explained that they were poor people, that she needed the car to drive to her nursing job at Riverside Hospital.

The romance of place said Pembroke's Arabian Horse Farm was sacred. Said there was a girl in these parts who was born to ride horses and there were horses born to listen to a girl who wore no spurs on her heels and whose fingers were the cradle of a lost and gentle logic. The romance of place was not allied to logic as you or I might know it. It repeated itself insistently. It said you can make an acre of memories as you can make a verb of horse, as you can horse any lexicon into beauty. Said although it has two eyes, a memory is a myopic animal with a square head. Said treacle is the honey lathered over time. Just as a big house surrounded by acres of pasture can be made to stand for something more than itself, a horse or car can come in the guise of a gift, that surplus of the giver's self, while in the ring the stapled ribbons flit and children learn to trot the serpentine, to care for what they can't afford to own.

The romance of place was my mother tugging on Tasha and Theron Pembroke's heartstrings by reciting a story about Molly and me as toddlers sitting on a pony named Pumpkin beneath the big oak tree in front of their farmhouse. The romance of place said I asked Pumpkin if she would be my horse when I grew up to be a cowboy. Said Molly told me Pumpkin was a pony, and I couldn't ride her anyway, I wasn't good enough, which was both true and mean, and when Mol-

ly was at her best, she was both true and mean. It was an apoc-
ryphal tale, likely based upon a photograph of the Shetland
my mother had spotted in the entranceway to the Pembrokes'
house. It was her way of wending us into the family's mem-
ory in hopes that we would stick. My mother's first theory of
posterity was that one must long be remembered with stories
false or true.

The Weather of Our Names

It wasn't exactly a meadow out there beyond the sliding door of my mother's parents' den but a large backyard, a double lot with plenty of space for children to play tag or catch, yet if you could excise the subdivision in imagination or at least blot the view of adjacent houses, you could picture an austere and endless meadow.

The erasure of the postwar subdivision on winter nights allowed one to picture the vestigial presence of the horse-drawn agrarian past that hadn't existed since Ford's quadricycle ride in 1898 began a process of industrialization that culminated in Eisenhower's interstate system. I-94 ribboned the snowy meadow just beyond the concrete retaining wall that did not retain the sound of the four cylinder and six cylinder engines from the Ford, Chevrolet, and Chrysler cars that sped along that deadly, unholy route save for when the winter weather came and cut down on the traffic and muted the noise of the extant traffic to a whisper that could have easily been mistaken for the snow falling through the branches.

I'm more interested in the sliding glass door in my memory than my maternal grandfather, William Hugh O'Neill, who sat before the door with the television perpetually running, who served with Merrill's Marauders in the China, Burma, and India Theater. One gets to the point rather quickly where people can't be known, where it's midnight and memory affords you the luxury of forgetting, or at least remembering selectively what was good about us. The point where there are no ideas but in place, and the love of place is a repudiation of its people.

To love any city or any once-meadow is maudlin. I'm incapable of loving what I've inherited but haven't earned. This is everything. Which is why I am so heartened by the transitory powers of the frames of sliding doors, the confusing but perfect mechanisms for locking down a house or cottage with what both clarifies and obfuscates a view.

When the sightline to the yard or lake is redacted by night's ink, the imagination awakens. The old man's cathode ray tube blue television light flickers like the wings of a bright jungle bird in the pane of glass behind him.

*

The house was a provisional space in the summertime. My grandmother, Gwendolyn Morrissey-O'Neill, would leave for the Dearborn Inn in the late morning to swim. She rarely actually swam. Grandma Gwen smoked and looked at the water, at the bathers in all their grotesque grace. She played bridge with friends beneath a Canadian maple tree. Gwen had a gift for imprecation. She once told me her children, including my mother, were sired by the devil. My father said he officially knew he was part of the family the day she called him a jackass. She instructed me more than once to never get into a pissing contest with a skunk. She was strong, tough, and tender, and she had a sense of social justice that was rare for a white suburban woman of her generation. I love that she hyphenated her name; bucking those patronymic conventions was incredibly subversive when she got married during the Eisenhower 1950s. She seemed ancient to me when she took me to the Dearborn Inn as a child, but she was only twenty years older than I am now.

Her death happened in March, but it felt like a cumulation of Augusts. Emphysema leading to congestive heart failure.

She doesn't visit me in dreams near my birthday anymore. One summer morning before we left for the pool, I took a lit cigarette from the pedestal ashtray in her kitchen and inhaled it; the smoke tasted to me like sand, or what I imagined sand would taste like.

Like an emphysemic lung, the house inhaled summer through its screen doors and window screens wadded up with paper napkins. What constitutes a summer beyond the thick months passing June to August? Hymenopterans wallowing in pollen, carbon burning off the macadam and asphalt, birds smacking their reflections in clear window panes, white moths arcing through thick air like poorly-struck golf balls, smoke.

My parents got married in that big backyard one June day in the late 1970s. My mother's parents hired a catering company to supply a pop-up bar and a tent with folding tables. Everybody drank, which was unremarkable, but my dad's dad came off the wagon that night after a long bout with sobriety. He never managed to catch back up to that slow-rolling horse-drawn coach, and he was exiled to his native Tulsa a few years later as a result, but he had a fine time celebrating the nuptials.

My paternal grandfather, my grandpa John, my namesake, was a quiet drunk; the only ones to notice him drinking were those who remembered he shouldn't have been drinking. I hardly knew him at all. I certainly knew him less than the grandfather who owned the house where the wedding took place, who owned the dog Eric and watched television in the midnight of half-sleep. When I was born, Grandpa John bought me a small stuffed bear from the gift shop on the ground floor of Henry Ford Hospital. John Calvin Freeman Senior was thrilled that my parents named me John Calvin Freeman III, and I'm glad that he found joy in this patronymical progression. Periodically my mother reminds me how happy my name made him when I complain about its ponderousness.

During the wedding reception, one of my mother's brothers walked through the sliding glass door, shattering the pane and slicing his forehead open. When he went to the hospital to get stitched up, he was too drunk for anesthesia, so they just sewed the stitches in his forehead and sent him back to the party. He plied himself with more beer without missing a beat. I think the fact that they had cleaned the pane of glass before the wedding had more to do with the mishap than my uncle's drunkenness. My uncle waded into the glass like a dumb bird blinded by what was clear.

My paternal grandfather, John Calvin Freeman Senior, stood back near the bar beneath the strings of lights and drank whiskey while listening to the far-off whoosh of traffic.

*

It's winter. I'm in Norton Shores, MI with my wife, Sarah Pazur (when we got married and she kept her maiden name, an iron worker friend of hers from childhood took to calling me "Big John Pazur," which I suppose was supposed to emasculate me but simply made Sarah and me laugh. We were also once quizzed by an American customs officer at the Detroit-Windsor border about how we could be married without sharing a last name. Some days I don't think our attitudes toward gender have progressed all that much since the lay of Ike). We're sharing a bottle of Stag's Leap Merlot. A gas fire sputters beneath the hearth, throwing little shadows of flame against the living room walls and against the sliding glass door that looks out at the inland sea. This house rests atop a parabolic sand dune. Lake Michigan banks sheets of ice against the ruined stairs that lead down to the erstwhile beach. Ice the color of dingy gulls spits up all over itself like a slack, atavistic maw.

I'm reading the Anna Livia Plurabelle episode in *Finnegan's Wake* and cataloguing references to Michigan bodies of water: An Sable, the Au Sable River that as a portmanteau echoes Anna Liffey and Anna Livia Plurabelle to evoke a river an ocean and a continent away; Joyce's version of Erie in its eutrophic period reads, *Bring about it to be brought about and it will be, loke, our lake lemanted, that great layck, the city of Is is issuant (atlanst!), urban and orbal, through seep froms umder unber great wasseres of Erie.* "Wasseres," like "wassail," a celebratory beverage or song, the bubbling algae of an industry's wake.

I have a theory about how Joyce knew the names of these Michigan lakes and tributaries that involves Hemingway's map of the Edenic bays and trout streams of his youth that he kept pinned above his writing desk in Paris in the 1920s when he was working through the Nick Adams stories. *Riverrun...* the *Wake* begins and, in its beginning, carries the virtues of its ending, a recursive, impossible book, a strange loop, *riverrun*, a portmanteau that functions both as noun and verb.

My father has just died at 70. I have just turned 41. I joke with people that I'm halfway to 82. I've been thinking a lot about mortality. My grandfather died at 60. My father took good care of himself and got 10 more years than his father. I live more like my grandfather than him.

I start to worry about the gas fire. Have I opened the flue? Am I breathing in carbon monoxide? I lie on my back and look up into the blackened chimney. The flue is open; the lightheadedness is from drinking. I walk over to the door and remove the wooden pole from the runner, sliding it open to the snow to hear the susurrations of the winter wind off Lake Michigan. Dense lake-effect snow, difficult to see through. Joni Mitchell's record *Blue* plays on Sarah's computer. I'm wondering about the accumulation of details in such a scene. She tells me to close the door, but I stand there for an extra beat or two, listening to the warble of that iconic voice disappear into the white. When snow blankets the world, it deadens our noise and lets us retreat into ourselves. February is a bad time to be mourning.

The other week I saw a video of George Plimpton interviewing Donald Barthelme. Barthelme said that he always forbade his students from writing about the weather. It made me think of the two-dimensional world of E.A. Abbott's *Flatland*, where no precipitation could fall from above, where geometry was transmuted into allegory. Looking out at the whiteout world beyond this dune, I understand the value in Barthelme's and Abbott's approach. The weather can be monotonous as grief. I close the door and jam the wooden pole back in the runner behind the doorframe. Part of me wants to be a line or a subnivean snow flea impaling nothing in a two-dimensional world. But the hypothetical is just as implausible as what happens. These constraints we place on the imagination are as oneiric as the dead who visit us in dreams.

Winter hangovers are more merciful than summer ones. The next morning we stand astride skis in a jack pine forest. We fall down. We leverage our poles to right ourselves. We gaze into a mess of boles putrefying in a muskeg and wonder if we can know the lake from its weather, its weather from the rimed riparian, ourselves from the thorny exigencies of the stories we inherit.

Even on days it doesn't snow, it comes in off the lake, lake effect, dust that falls for hours, isolating us in the clamor of our thoughts. For the bluffs of these dunes are colder than the surface of the water, and the snow is quieter than anything I think, its sheer ascent enacts a convection as uncanny as our names.

*

The dog Eric watches birds in the backyard on a summer afternoon. We are fifteen minutes west of Detroit. My mother's father sits in the armchair watching Tigers baseball on the TV. It's 1987. Frank Tanana is pitching. The crafty lefthander grew up in Detroit throwing 90+ MPH smoke, but by the time he returned to our hometown he'd cultivated an assortment of change-ups, curveballs, and screw balls that he could locate with pinpoint accuracy to keep hitters off-balance. Tanana is rain falling through the leaves of a paper birch and petrichor through a screen door. My grandfather watching Tanana while I watch the dog watch birds is rain falling through the leaves of a paper birch and petrichor through a screen door. Woven aluminum and rain, an impending rain delay fifteen minutes east into the future. The west is the future if we follow the path of the sun, but the east is the future of the storms of this peninsula. I have tarped the field of this remembrance. The elders who loved me enough to keep me safe from weather stand below their porticoes in a perpetual rain delay. Tanana throws softly against a dugout wall to keep his arm loose in case the game resumes.

My father told the story of watching *A Long Day's Journey Into Night* in this den before he and my mother were married. My grandmother had gone upstairs to bed, and my grandfather, though he slept in the armchair in the den, followed after her to check the doorknobs on the upstairs bedroom doors, some ritual or superstition he performed each night while the rest of the house went quiet. My mother's father's name was William Hugh O'Neill, named after Hugh O'Neill, the Earl of Tyrone, who fought against the Tudors in Ireland during the Nine Years' War. I have to think Eugene O'Neill had the very same figure in mind when he named his father James Tyrone in the thinly-fictionalized play. *The Encyclopedia of Baseball,* a big hardcover book with every statistic in the game up to 1984 printed in its pages sat on the magazine stand next to his chair, though I don't think my grandfather ever read it.

Rain skulks through the I-94 corridor and wafts through the aluminum screen as it heads toward the ballpark to postpone Tanana's start. Postponement, punishment for bombast, tacit admission that we have no agency in planning. What does it mean to excise the weather from what we have written? Only in a weatherless narrative do we exert any real control. The snow accumulates substance. The rain erodes what we have built upon, the open-aired pastime bares our habits to the contingencies of fate. My grandfather takes a Welch's popsicle from the freezer in the kitchen and watches as the 34 year old deceives another hitter with a parabolic curveball that no one sane could hit.

*

Last time I was in Norton Shores, my father was still alive. He was 69 and I was a day past 40 wandering a rain-slicked pier on Lake Michigan named for the French Jesuit priest Pere Marquette, my eyes red with weather and the previous night's wine. A murder of crows bleated in the sand. The wind muffled the details of their plaints. Black-jacketed, officious, they could've been celebrants in a corvid rite for all I knew. The tennis-shoe-white spinnaker on the horizon didn't seem to move, taut with cross-hatching winds, the boat stuck inside a late-autumn convection.

A pier's no place for perseverant lovers to promenade, its wayfinding enhanced by horns and beacons as if to tell us, indisputably, that geography is impervious to mission and no legend can convert the combers into knots, no keel unknot them. It's a place you come to alone, if you come at all.

Here's an allegory, then: Our man on the peninsula staggers the last third of the rabble in the cold, blind spray while the paper birches shed yellow leaves in a northeast gale. It's no place for a peripatetic drunk, but who isn't fooled into thinking these peninsulas will last, who has the courage to see the little animal of the self as liminal?

Joliet, Marquette's friend and colleague, variegated and blue-black with bruises, ventured out in a birch bark canoe on this lake to joyfully ply his paddles in 1673; his diary was destroyed (thick book, sallow pages scalloping in river water) leaving only Marquette's bloodless, fastidious account of forging a new path down the Meskousing. *Thus we left the waters flowing to the Quebog, 4 or 500 leagues from here to float on those that would thenceforward take us to strange lands. Before embarking theron, we began all together a new devotion to the blessed Virgin Immaculate,* Marquette wrote as they entered the mouth of the Mississippi.

Out of fear, they didn't go all the way to the Gulf. The Menominee forebodings about river monsters, Fire People, and Spaniards didn't come true though; instead, Marquette died of dysentery off the coast of Ludington on his way back to the Jesuit mission at Saint Ignace. He was 37, old enough to know that what little we learn from our travels can't be reasonably applied at home, that only in pelts and palaver can someone be converted. That once the missionaries leave, their strange words decohere like vision in sandspit. That what we call grace is only safety owed to happenstance, a fluke.

You might think this is the price of hubris, but who isn't befuddled by the grandiosity of humble intent? Who isn't fooled into thinking these waters can be charted, that our riparian friendships can be real, that posterity can be capsuled in a name? Who doesn't feel the living name outlive us; who is ordained to bless these swollen shores?

A rainbow arced over the harbor. Crumbling wooden stairs dangled precariously above the breakwater at the foot of the bluff. Last year's woven straw from a bird's nest, the remnant of a home, tumbled down the beach. Marram grass thinned on a nape of dune, and my skull only felt like a parabola of sand as listless crows combed through the day after the day of the anniversary of my birth.

*

Everyone knew why my mother's father didn't sleep through the night, though no one talked about it. They all knew why the banality of pat reruns comforted him. I think I know why he gazed into that television set as the Tigers or golf tournaments or episodes of *Matlock* played. I imagine my parents' wedding in that backyard, the storm clouds gathering in the humid June air passing over the festivities without opening into deluge. *The rain held off*, as we like to say in the Midwest.

My mother tells the story about the time her father fell asleep with a cigarette in his left hand and accidentally set the couch on fire. When he woke up and saw the cushions aflame, he opened the sliding door and dispassionately tossed the whole couch on the patio before going back to sleep.

My mother claims he read *Gravity's Rainbow* during a string of insomniac TV-watching nights and says he was fascinated by the supersonic V-2 rockets featured in the book, how they arrived like derechos, only offering audible warning after their destruction was done. When my mother was a girl, the shed behind the house was blown away by straight-line winds, one of those bottle-green Midwestern storms that develop in the summer. The concrete slab upon which the shed stood bore a rust parallelogram outline and the misshapen handprints of fallen birch and maple leaves long after it was gone.

Disambiguation With Barry Sanders, Pluto, and Persephone

My sister holds her dead dog's leash. Her pale hands grip the braided pink fabric. She flicks the light end unconsciously; the heavy end with the steel collar clip hangs from her right hand like an anchor.

"It's gonna be a hard day," she says.

"Every white-knuckled day is hard," I almost tell her.

How tone-deaf, these thoughts. I don't think the dog ever recognized or remembered me, growling and barking each time I approached her house.

I'm trying to remember if Odysseus's dog was named Argos or Arcturos as my sister holds her dead dog's leash.

*

This morning I woke up to the Muskegon River cloaked in fog, my breath stale from last night's wine, and I didn't remember where I was right away. I flipped on the TV to a story about the new Barry Sanders statue outside Ford Field, the entirety of the eight-foot bronze likeness balanced on the right toe to capture his dexterity and elusiveness, how he could evade tacklers even when the opposing defense sniffed out the play.

Barry said it was very lifelike, pointing out how sculptors Ori Amrany and Lou Cella included his trademark fingerless gloves. Lifelike—not the fingers wrapped around the ovoid sphere but the gloves.

If we are not what we are but what we do, then we are also the tools we employ in the doing, I think.

How did you get through, Barry Sanders, when their 5-2 front was assembled? Is it that greatness is impervious to strategy? Are we always only what we used to be?

Or was it pure improvisation, an ineffable gift? Is that why you went about your work so quietly, never spiking the ball, calmly handing it off to the referee after every touchdown?

*

Last night I dreamed my sister was driving her dog to Bishop Park in my father's old teal Ford Festiva, a ridiculous car for anyone but especially for my 6'4" father. I've always mixed up Argos and Arcturos, but the bright star reflected off the Detroit River. I've always mixed up Argos and Arcturos, but the dimwitted dog reflected in the river couldn't see itself.

Emily, what is the meaning of this dream? That we seek quaint downtowns with peaceful water vistas when the usual spectacles won't do?

My sister pointed at the star in the water and said, "Pluto."

*

The only time I saw Barry Sanders play was Mike Utley's tragic final game at the Pontiac Silverdome. I was there with my uncle and my father. Utley gave a thumbs-up when they carried him off the field on a stretcher. Spinal fracture. He hasn't walked since. I was reminded of this watching former coach Wayne Fontes speak of Barry's humble approach and otherworldly talent.

The putative story of that team is that they galvanized around tragedy and overcame it, winning their division and the franchise's lone playoff game. Sounds like rah-rah drivel. Sounds like the vicissitudes of family life.

*

Before I learned about the solar system in school, I associated Pluto solely with the cartoon dog. I Google "facts about Pluto" and read of its disputed planetary status, its failure to clear its orbit. It's a dwarf or minor-planet, sharing a path with millions of small icy bodies in the Kuiper Belt.

I try to contrast this fact with the way Barry Sanders was able to harness gravity, to hurtle out of the backfield and zig-zag through the secondary until nothing was before him except latitudinal white lines leading to the end zone's silver and blue horizon.

Maybe only in sports or art do we think of elusiveness as a positive quality. "Elusive" sounds like "Eleusinian," that set of mysteries and rites, and in this world, Pluto is the stern elusive God of Hades, husband of Persephone. I don't call her enough; I know my late father would want us to be closer.

*

They project a still of the statue leaping from its pedestal. As it was in 1991, as it isn't now, and ever shall be. He said the detail of the fingerless gloves brought him to tears when he first saw it. "It's puzzling what ends up getting to us and making us cry," he said. He never expected it to hit him that way.

III.

Yelping the Huron River Inn

A wreath can be good if you're walking north
or if you simply spot it on a neighbor's door
across the road. Headlights can also be good
for a mind perpetually flowing south.
I don't try to overdo it, that stuff that stultifies the tongue.
It's fearful boredom; they've left me alone with
asphalt and concrete unspooling.
I've never ended up anywhere better after driving,
but still I drive. Another wreath, this time on a transept,
this time wired to a soffit.
I've heard the mourning doves
that once populated it. People in these parts
are quick to tell you not to follow
Huron River Road past where the river bends
lest you land in Rockwood.
There's a real night out there and a cold sky
whose celestial bodies glint.
A mill pond nauseated by the moon in water,
a jack pine stand behind a Taco Bell,
brown scrub oaks along the highway.
I've been in this business a long time,
long enough to know the price of a wreath
full of replica tanagers from the free whiskey shot
they give when the cargo train crosses the bridge
outside the window of the Huron River Inn
where twin spruces tower before
the knotty pine door, iron boar's nose
for a knocker, needles on the sidewalk
plashing beneath your shoes.

Disambiguation With a Dead Carp on the Bank

Unplayable tennis court, its serving boxes blue with mud and cracking paint.
A hyperborean bent to the wind today.
I can't warm up to the wiki they've made of my breath.
I'm hyperlinked to carp and sunshine. The rain rolling in
looks like a smoky valence, while the rain falling down is reticular as mesh.
I'm different from my father, my eponym.
I think you and others would like me to be like him,
but I really can't approximate his intelligence or patience.
I'm more of an amalgam character, at best.
His worst dog, a big, dumb lab mix,
had no compunctions about pissing into the weather
or eating trash. I'm more like that. O Lord,
sometimes I think it's cruel to ask us to sleep beneath the stars
and taste the gin that comes from heaven as the ice melts.
I've never understood the phrase, *Long in the tooth*,
except as a way to signify what a rat that's gnawed on nothing
must endure. I've been a lost ball in tall weeds,
distaff of a careless volley, a pint bottle
chucked into the creek. North or northerly, I don't have to tell you
what purposelessness can't do. I practice only vague attribution
when the current season does not foretell the next.
Somebody says the cut leaves are a library of past autumns.
Somebody says yellow is the death of the brick-and-mortar school.
Somebody calls the river a creek, but no one can deny the beauty
of fallen honey locust leaves in still black water.
A turkey vulture lofts atop its shadow,
its bald head a spindle in the sky.
I refuse to be what putrefies in sallow light;
I bow my head to the fish our friends have come for.

Tender Years: A Brief Memoir
With *Eddie and the Cruisers*

A season by its weather swaps our footwear
and our garments as we travel snow-swept roads
without volition. This is what it means to tremolo
and slide. Nobody lives up to their memoirs;
no story can remain accurate once it's set down.
Call it the always-evanescent present, call it
time passed before it's arrived, call it self-mythology,
the putrefying masque of the persona, taillights
tailing off in epistrophe—call this carnelian,
collodion of nightfall—young John, dumb bag
of bones riding that stretch of Ike's interstate
between Allen Park and Marshall in his parents'
Escort wagon—call it an exculpatory metaphor
for how the self is interpellated *a priori* by
an ideological interstate apparatus, call it a parody
of Althusser, call it a staid middle class epistle.
He lies on the backseat, the chairs collapsed,
and watches *Eddie and the Cruisers* on a 12"
TV/VCR combo plugged into the cigarette lighter
while herds of deer peek out of weeds in roadside culverts—
call it distantiation of the self from self, palinode
of an early maunder. Pale as moonlight, skinny
as a wicket John, bag of bones, and why
was that film made, and why was he watching it
on his way past shelterbelts and maze fields turned
the blue of dusk, late autumn, single stoplight towns
with gas stations and landbound kettle lakes
and porn shops advertising "live peep shows"
and party stores advertising "live nightcrawlers."
Call it the vomitous underbelly of the rural idyll
or something pithier than that if you think of it.
He learns the word "caesura," he learns the name

"Rimbaud," learns the anaphora of anaphora of songs—
that a life is a set of cylindrical structures for those
beyond us to decode. In the film the music's mostly diegetic—
Chevy Bel Air dangling from the Raritan Bridge
in the morning rain while "Wild Summer Nights"
implausibly plays on its radio. In a classroom in Ocean City,
Frank Ridgeway (Tom Berenger), the bandmember
they called "The Word Man," is puzzling over
"Lines Composed a Few Miles Above Tintern Abbey"
while flashing back to a moment playing "Tender Years"
on a baby grand on some bandstand in Atlantic City,
and is this diegetic, happening as it does twenty years remote
from the empty classroom where he dreams? Call it
the polemic against music in real time, call it the irrefutable
oneiric quality of song. Every poem is a persona poem,
a friend will tell our passenger many years later, and if this is true,
every poem is a palinode of a self worn down to its seams
in ventriloquy and maunder, which means we'll never know
who Eddie Wilson or Arthur Rimbaud really were while knowing
that no one really is anyone once the credits roll.
John Cafferty's soundtrack was criticized for its anachrony
(the band was from the early 60s but Cafferty sounded
like 80s Springsteen). *Do people change or don't they,
that's what Wordsworth's getting at,* Ridgeway says.
For the longest time he heard it as "words worth getting at,"
not an author name but a question of emphasis—anaphora,
epistrophe, refrain. When Eddie Wilson comes back,
a reflection watching his younger self in a cathode ray tube
TV in the display front of an appliance store, his ensuing visitations
to former band members offer an answer our passenger holds onto
hopelessly. Call it stumbling the parapets of before,
the putative before. A man watches himself watching his former self,
a Bel Air dangles from a bridge rail, every poem is a persona poem
just as every resurrection, every film, every happy accident
involves some meticulous, doubtful possibility—a recovered
reel-to-reel, a missing stone, a living ghost.

Yelping Ford Lanes

It's not clear to the layperson
how a bowling league works,
but yes, there's a hell
in these peoples' minds.
Three straight turkeys,
nary a perfect game.
She thought of her mother
frothing at the mouth
the day she died and saying,
Tell them I was a nurse. Nurse.
Not the mother. Not a mother.
Never a mother.
Nary a mother but this creature
with a marsupial's jaw
sibylline in wasting.
She thought of other things.
Suddenly she was the last woman
in an alley grown terribly quiet.
They were hammering at a chest
thrown into a contrapuntal rhythm,
hammering against dire facts
with a dire procedure
in a dire time of the year.
That's nine frames of perfection.
Tortuous to get that close.
She would approach the line,
step each heel to each toe four times,
and deliver. It's hard to clearly
draw the empire of the unborn
she palmed in her black sphere,
but she had the ability
to hear them be not-nothing

before they slipped away.
She could almost remember a time
when pinsetters worked
in that odd penumbra
between the dark and light.

Tomorrow Fries An Egg

and plates it to demonstrate
how rapidly a memory congeals.

Tomorrow's memory is alimentary.
Tomorrow's breakfast is something else.

Tomorrow, full of hail and laughter,
drives its clipper down the interstate to Flat Rock.

Tomorrow strums a song in poplar leaves;
it flushes mallards from the burdock.

Tomorrow makes a vocative of sand
and stomps the hardened pellets from our shoes.

Tomorrow buys the green bananas.
Tomorrow is adept at waiting.

Tomorrow is the edge wave of a seiche
breaking cattail stalks like matchsticks.

Tomorrow arrows over a barrier island
like a tern—its eyes scan the water.

Tomorrow is a basket on a bicycle
carrying buttermilk and green bananas.

Tomorrow asks the pickerel to unhook its maw;
it has no stomach for what's foretold in putrefaction.

Tomorrow kites astride the turkey buzzard;
its guts are sour. It's halfway to 82.

Disambiguation With Firetrucks at Elsinore

One day, you'll have died fat and happy,
bloated cheeks caked in make-up to animate your face;
there's nothing vatic in saying this in future tense.

You've seen the confetti of shelled tickets
at the Northville Downs harness races,
that brand of faith in mud and whips

and numbers has mercifully fallen out of style.
My aunt says at three-score and ten it's difficult
to reconcile time and place when I text her happy birthday.

She's reading Shakespeare in Cross Village
beside Lake Michigan. I can hear doppler sirens elongated
by a quarter-mile of distance. A neighbor of a neighbor

says there are men high in the silver maples behind her
house.
This has happened to her before. My wife saw a number 3
helium balloon in the woman's tree today.

When one is mad we say *Out of their tree.*
The synoptic gospels never had to invent anything
for Christ to do, but without that episode

at the wedding party in the book of John, I doubt
anyone would care as much. It's the wine,
not the purgation or transubstantiation we hold

apocryphal and dear. My wife loves the elegant recursion
of the number 3, how it overtakes the civic mind.
A neighbor of a friend and neighbor

seems to be going mad. The neighborhood, solicitous
to a fault, hangs onto this digit so full of helium's
ambitions. What gets restrained and wheeled away

is a who imbued with a buoyant mystery.
The fire department can't seem to find
the men in the trees; it's not for lack of vision.

Yelping Heck's Bar

Bean fields on a till plain in the thumb
of Michigan. "Heck's Bar" in majuscule
of chipped letters on a warped brick face.
Whose booths are reinforced with electrical tape,
whose pool table molders beneath a sanguine
Budweiser chandelier, cues crooked,
felt slow as sand, talc scurf at the teak
base of a teak spindle, CD jukebox against the wall
with all anybody's desired these last forty years
printed on placards in small block Helvetica.
Where behind a Formica plank stands
Robert Heck Jr. who knows Fox River
in the UP was the river described
in the Hemingway story but not the river
after which they named the story and the beer
he keeps on tap. The beer here pours well
too, the taps cleaned bi-weekly.
A trout stream's flow and pooling, a bi-chambered
elegance in naming or misnaming.
Heck, I say, and he starts to laugh, whose namesake
and father once ran as a Republican for sheriff
of these parts (I first wrote, *Whose father
was a state senator from these parts*
before realizing he was mostly less than that),
whose grain elevator across the gravel parking lot
still holds the vestiges (square cinderblock structure
beneath the silo, concrete countertop,
brass footrail, gilt Hamm's mirror
greening near the bottom) of the first
family bar, says his dad would know
exactly what to think about today's
political talk, which I take as an endorsement.

The four humors in me are misaligned,
the yellow bile high around the eyes and sclera.
In a framed picture propped against a promotional
bottle of blended Canadian whiskey,
Heck and all his regulars, yokel smiles
beneath neatly-trimmed goatees, are half-ringed
around a cardboard cutout of the former president.
I finish the remaining bites of my olive burger,
swig the last of the Two Hearted in my pint glass,
think of cast-off trout with scorches of fingerprints
on their scales, pay my tab, and leave.
As I pull out of the gravel lot, the sky over West Kinde
Road goes dark with a summer storm—petrichor,
then dust to mud splat on green leaves.
Covetous but loyal, Heck stands back there
with the patriarch lionized in repetition, Ixion
who could have easily been Menelaus
or Paris, whose appetites whet to temperaments
that say, *Our times are only of our time.*
I'll have a pint of Two Hearted and an olive
burger, medium. Back at the cabin on Saginaw Bay,
I sit on a small deck in a copse of trees
and wonder if I use the word "copse" too much
and further wonder what difference it would make
if I denied myself this pleasure.
A trumpeter swan outstretches its wings
before a bevy. It's good to live a brief evening
where swans whose plumage won't come clean
in photographs are not embodiments of gods.
Needless instinct, no dignity in the way they fight
and frolic down the isthmus off the point.

Must We on the Way to the Island

In memory of a boy drowned in the Grosse Ile Canal in 1987

Hear the song of drowned Krenshaw,
a song that has no words, adumbrations
of ice along a scrim of shore.
I remember the waterspout on Lake Erie
one July evening decades ago,
the plaited grey sky against
the tail of grey menacing
what weakened it—land, gaze, breath—
malaise, that mechanism
for seeing the evident in grief, bedevils
the old innocence. The old innocents
took a hammer to the ice to test it
before crossing the canal. Krenshaw's mother
leaves traces of kisses on the filters
of Virginia Slims. She has no appetite
for seasons. I've only loved
the Christ child to the nether points
of accountability, I want to tell her.
There's no reason to believe
in rebirth from this dank bedding
when you have an unabated Manitoba
slicing at your favorite thicket
and Hermes again slicing at the throat
of mist—psychopomp, Escort
whose tires the grates of the drawbridge
pull for a closer look over the rail
where Krenshaw lives.

Yelping the Bella Vista

You're staying in Room 8. You like it here, despite the musty smell. You can watch the lake from the picnic table on the patio. "Bella Vista" is spelled out in bold cursive on the concrete bottom of the pool. It feels good to say it aloud—*Bella Vista*, beautiful view, grand view. It doesn't translate perfectly, but you look out and there's Lake Huron's Saginaw Bay; it's ocean-blue or blue as the sky or blue as what we maim in our descriptions. The waves this evening are whitecapped combers that spray the support bars of the jet ski lift before collapsing in a despondent clop in the sand. They haven't hosted weddings at the Bella Vista in years, but they still advertise this service on every room door. *Of all the marriages doomed to failure, why have so many of the profligate befriended me?* seems like a question for the shuttered ballroom or a prescient epithalamium. Is it something other than doom that keeps the vows coming but not keeping? A tacit understanding that ten good years beats ten lonely ones? The wisdom of knowing that forever is a concept which, despite our formal histrionics, can never be convincingly acted out? Weddings are soliloquys; marriages are more than that. A steel swingset is anchored in the breakwater. Kid Rock blares from someone's Bluetooth speaker. You want to say it doesn't sound like here, but how could it not sound like here? You're somewhere south of the Big Dipper, unsure if that makes sense. The lone maple soughs in humid air. The shouting next door's become rhapsodic. Drunks cloak themselves in noise, but it's really more akin to resignation. Too late for apology or grace. The gone years, the wasted calligraphy and crepe. You step into a swing and boomerang over the water. You think it might be Tawas across the bay. You went to a wedding there once that took place behind a little blue cottage on the banks of the Au Sable. Now they've sold the place and split the money. *Nothing really ends,* you think, looking out across the lake and knowing otherwise. Shadow of a pier in the light of a buoy that tells you you're returning to something: song, place, or figment. Superior mirage, lights, refraction, inversion of air masses revealing the impossible—a buoyant city, a levitating ship.

Disambiguation With One Bird in the Hand

To be just gone, to be
gone as you are just
adjusting to the old house,
your fellow creatures
and the soft light
around the lamp.
To refuse to listen
to a querulous voice
whose only intention
is to soothe and keep you
on this earth. Do you trust
yourself to cradle
a small creature in your hands
and quell its better instincts,
which is to say
assuage its fear? If no,
you shouldn't own a bird.
Your father never did.
Now he's as ethereal
as the enamel the anti-seizure
drug Tegretol leached from
your sister's teeth.
You remember
how she vomited
against the windshield
of that '76 Mercury Cougar
the day he dropped her
on her head. He's not alive
in that stairwell,
but you can find part of him
living there. He's the only one
who blamed him for that fall.

The white parakeet
she bought after his death
perched on her wrist
for the first time today,
then it escaped and flew
lividly around the room.
Let there be a lesson
in a bird refusing its cage,
but don't turn it into allegory.
The only worthwhile
lessons are narrowly
applied. What kind
of sad bastard
buys a bird to fill
a void? What kind
of void is filled
by imprecation?
You're also seeking
the affection that animals
can't offer. You're glad
he's in Flat Rock
in a crypt six feet
above the ground,
down the road
from the pie shop
where he'd sip piping
hot black coffee
and read Hart Crane
while listening to
the whine and tremolo
of cargo trains, next to
the southern bank
of that quiet forking river.
You loaded his ashes
into the vault

on the day of his internment
because no one else
had the stomach for it.
A crypt is not a cage,
though it too is for
your own good.
To be that lithe,
to perch upon a hand
and feel the tremor
carry through
the hollow legs.

Under the Tegmine

The hermit crab
leaves everything
to leave no trace but
that blue peripatetic
squatter's husk
in sand, nothing
in the shell, the shell
another crustacean's
home that was lost
and borrowed.
We all become
such menacing
little figures
with our plague years
behind us.

~

Saltwater digitigrade, what's the occasion for remembering?

The tin-eared, mystifying clang of a pantoum,

the ostensible profundity in repetition?

~

Bipedalism is a state
conducive to moving
through the canopies of trees,
yet our gilded selves
on terra firma ornament
the sand with filigree

and sketches. The modes
of writing that have killed
off the old modes miss
their vestigial selves
to the same extent a retriever
misses hind dewclaws
and fore dewclaws
in the marshes when it rains.
Can I ask you a question
is a question I've asked
many times without permission.

~

She left you her books,
her sextant,
her Nikon Aculon binoculars.
So don't forget to tell
your loved ones
about the awful thing
that will obliviate
their beliefs.
Yes, say, say yes
at Rogers Pond
we were so happy
watching an osprey
release the pickerel
it had killed
for the floating mass
of carrion birds to work on.
They were of a single
mind that bickered
only with itself.

Those Vacation Plans You Made

A gull perches on an edge of polished shale
surveying the reef for minnows.
Port Hope is a cruel name
for a beleaguered fishing village,
Sarah says when you suggest driving there
for dinner. The gull spears a small bass
and flies away. You think of what has shuddered,
then shuttered, crumbling facades
and waspy soffits clogged with paper nests,
the mordant elegance of the hexacomb,
while telling yourself you don't believe
in hopelessness. A boat ride to Turnip Rock,
a stack island made of limestone, the shadows
of its resident red pines elongating
and recoiling like a harpist's fingers
as the afternoon goes on.
The old truths should be easier to say.
You can't pray to your mother
or your father the way you can
to a windward stretch of bay
overburdened by the sunlight.
Lake Huron gets more and more prosaic
as clear days accrue (blue the quality
of the troposphere, powder-blue),
but then the future seems to bow
to you, its precarious sandstone barques
calving from the peninsula,
last winter's ice floes still shaping
this shoreline in July. It's a problem
of tense, not time. If the bay
didn't preserve its many wrecks,
there'd be nothing to dive for but an experience

of water. Back at the cottage, an oak leaf
jammed in sand looks like a cockatrice
or sphinx with its own set of arcane riddles.
The swells left you seasick
in addition to being drunk today.
The mind must long for gone places
when the body cannot visit,
the kinds of places the imagination
concocts when the kinds of places
you once loved have shuttered.
You'll drive to the Port Hope Hotel,
in other words, just as tomorrow
you'll drive downstate to sing
a song at Linda's funeral.
But first perch at the Port Hope,
then a shot and beer at the Buccaneer,
then back to the cabin for wine and music.
First, then falls out of sequence,
as you narrate what won't row
parallel to shore in kayaks
or plash in breakwater on rafts.
There's no such thing as a peninsula
when you're drinking and listening
to Joni Mitchell's *Blue* in pitch darkness.
Nobody else should sing this one,
she'll say as "Little Green" comes on.
Tomorrow you'll rip the shoulder
of your sportscoat while bending forward
to pull on your socks. You'll realize
she forgot her funeral dress at home.
You'll sing "Little Green" in a cathedral
and cry with Linda's daughters,
but first you'll return to that crepuscular hour
before eulogy and song
when the towns across the bay

threw mini-replicas of themselves
into the water, the hour of swifts
and swallows, the hour when the pier
of Standish and two red buoys
debuted in a wash of rain.

Yelping Portofino Restaurant

Where stone coves and peaks beneath the earth,
a lightless plain unfurls like a strait. Sci-fi writer and lunatic
Richard Sharpe Shaver, in the Arkansas Ozarks, was able

to believe in an emptiness both habitable and lightless,
along with restive figures he called "deros" who rose
periodically from Hollow Earth to torture us.

I was able to believe something akin to this
while considering a recent spate of drownings and watching
the Detroit River current flow around the point at Elba Island.

Impending solstice, Thanksgiving brunch, the day dark
before it was over. At Portofino, we'd eat shrimp scampi,
drink New Zealand Sauvignon Blanc, and watch the water.

A swift span of water, when viewed from a tall window
or dock, can cleanse the heart and mind, and a holiday brunch
is preferable to a plated dinner in a house

that backs up to the woods. Yet where water ribbons
over itself in a narrow channel, a quiet muffles even
the bearer of curdling blood. An unhappy woman

swam out and didn't return, a boy fell from his dock,
a priest was thrown from a boat by a rogue wave.
We cannot know ourselves in time, I heard him

preach once in a sleepy church off of Brest Bay.
To rely on the lifespan of a restaurant to outlast ours,
to get even a few of us together every holiday over a span

of decades… Robin said the first thing she thought of
when she heard the place was closing was the time Louise puked
on the Easter Bunny. I'm not sure why small children

are so scared of the Easter Bunny, ermine in its whiteness,
but I think that particular Easter Bunny may have been a dero,
along with the men and women lurking behind

the buffet line in crepe hats serving food with tongs.
There's a fervor for reconfiguring our spaces inherited,
Shaver would argue, from the ancient civilizations

of Hollow Earth, from darkling plains and narrow channels
in the blood. Perhaps another restaurant will open
on the site, but we'll have our reasons not to go there.

Words for Port Austin

The waxing crescent moon's an open paren where any anecdote might fit. You think you're thinking but those mechanisms are gummed like the orb weaver's ticks. This cloying sense of the real we measure every experience against—the blue bird and the swan in the back dune swale do not seem real.

I get an email from the writer RS Deeren. He grew up in Caro, Michigan, and said he never really saw anyone else writing about Michigan's Thumb but told me he had swum in the Pinnebog River and eaten ice cream at Grindstone as a boy.

I tell him I hiked the trail behind The Buccaneer Den this morning. Its dusty windows are peppered with "No Parking" and "No Trespassing" signs.

One of the few extant Yelp reviews of the place comes from Jennie S. and reads, "The elderly workers were rude and did not want us there. They actually made us get our own menu off someone's table (yes, while they were eating). The elderly bartender spilled my drink, bringing it to me half-full.

I was sitting at the bar, not a table. Didn't offer to refill it. I asked several other questions about Port Austin and apparently I was bothering them." This used to be a supper club, and in the afternoon anglers would bring their catches to sell or have them cleaned and fried on site.

The pin oaks have ampersands for leaves and roots that go on and on in polysyndeton. The benefit of boarded-up rural supper clubs with scabbed-up motel pools abutting state lands stitched with hiking trails leading to scenic vistas above lakes is that even those who were never in the business of marram

grass can imagine the succession of small ecosystems culmi-
nating in the ominous shadows of scrub oak.

This afternoon I watched a tractor uproot jet ski lifts from
shallow water. It marked the end of a season that never really
was. I snap a picture on my phone and caption it, *You can't see
the lights of Standish from a beach head in Port Austin because
there are no lights in Standish.* It only becomes a beach head
if we think of dusk as a militaristic advance.

Crows at the shoreline, or maybe grackles, a swan so white
and hyperreal against the blue it looks ornamental. I refuse to
say the swan's a trumpeter; it sounds political, and, like you,
I'm dealing with a plurality of morons who look for blazons of
sun on water, which I also do, who comment on the breadth
of the beach this year, which I also do. The water is low, and
we have ten extra feet of sand. I won't say, *All littorals are false,*
for fear of where the metaphor might go.

The beach is an obscene place, and no obscenity can be con-
strued as false. The glistening breadth of sand, the high-water
scum of last year's flotsam before the seawall, a man blowing
hopelessly into a pair of water wings (once I realized nothing
had ever been innocent I kept on writing about what had yet
to happen to the self in a notational, atemporal parenthetical
I hadn't planned on including). I won't say I have heroes, but
if I did, they would be writing *Sleepless Nights* and quoting
Aeschylus.

Somebody should buy the Buccaneer and rehab it, fix up the
motel, bring up singers from Detroit every weekend like they
used to. I watch a girl take a large plastic shovel to a mound
of sand and shape it into the likeness of a castle. Moon in a
daytime sky, stand of paper birches on a tombolo bayed at by
the bay, a reflection the tide-less weight of here won't close.

Fair Lane

Gold scum on the pond in the Clara B. Ford Rose Garden.
The tin roof of the tea pavilion creaks.
Yew hedges train themselves to the limestone wall,
and the low-gradient river babbles where those "vagabonds"
Henry Ford, Thomas Edison, John Burroughs
and Harvey Firestone rowed and discussed strategies
for coaxing the proletariat (they wouldn't have used that term)
to give up alcohol, meat, and jazz, to exercise the morals
requisite for self-improvement.
I'm less intent on history these days.

For now it's enough to stroll the thicketed walkways
of Jens Jensen's mind and emerge in the long evening light
of the meadow. To live in a town riddled with eponyms
of such a man could be a source of bitterness and the raspberry
brambles *do* look bitter and the yews look bitter and the rip rap
scrabbling up the berm looks bitter, and the bitter geese,
they hiss and plash in vernal pools. The yews were planted
with no thought for the hunger marchers of 1932 or the workers
beaten on the overpass in 1937 by Harry Bennett's pigs.

We ascend the stone steps in the shade of tamaracks,
pick phragmites with wobbling blades on their stems—
this riverain, untenable riparian, these invasive prepositions
taking us from noun to noun like rhizomes, this slow green water
healing itself of decades—from the mortar they degrade,
then head down the trail over the warped pedestrian bridge to our car
with the iconic blue oval on its grill.
A moped with no lights tears down the avenue
in a cloud of smoke and a stench of burning oil.

Why put the world on wheels and mourn the world paved over?

Why wring nostalgia from the Dearborn sky as the river floods?
Why bother growing old in opulence?
The mansion must curate itself rainlessly when the weeks go rainless,
must drive its innocent tourists into the dark with floodlights
after dusk, must wait out the craven patriarch
when his ghost neglects its visitations.

Yelping Echo's

The quality of the perch isn't why
a restaurant succeeds or fails, but I miss
the pan-fried perch at Echo's. Fresh Lake Erie perch,
lightly breaded, a recipe the family would never divulge
when I asked them. I never caught their names,
but I feel awful they didn't make it.
When I was a kid, this place
was called Chaim Sweeney's and
Charlie Taylor used to sing here (there?),
and unless you heard him do
"The Wild Colonial Boy" and "The Flower
of Sweet Strabane," you likely have no affinity
for the building. Affixing new names
to buildings without structurally changing them
does a lot for ambiance though.
It gives an architecture to memories real
and imagined, personal or channeled
from the muddled anachrony of décor,
the palimpsestic layering of linoleum and wallpaper.
Chaim Sweeney was the world's foremost authority
on the hamburger, the menu said,
and I wouldn't blame anyone for thinking
this was bombast since the hamburgers
at the eponymous restaurant were unremarkable.
I'd ride in the backseat of my grandmother's Ford Escort wagon
down Outer Drive, that high curving road
commissioned by the WPA
to ribbon the perimeter of Detroit,
that uncompleted road, that floodplain
tracing the southern bend of the cantankerous Ecorse River,
to hear old Charlie sing. He'd let me sit at the edge
of the stage and strum Irish rebel songs

on my plastic guitar during his breaks.
Chaim Sweeney pissed his money
out the door on live entertainment,
which is ostensibly an enticement
to draw beer drinkers in,
but Echo's was doomed at the naming.
I think of Echo's story and a

                    caterwaul of the gone rings out
                       drowns the preening boy
              and lifts him off in the face of half-voiced
                                     predation
                    he was not so special they never are
         she chattered nonsensically during Jove's trysts
                      to slow Juno's pursuit deleted
                      all prefixes muted vocatives
              the effect only approximating the sound
                     of sound returning she clutched
                            the leaning putrefaction
                   the boy in putrefaction in tableau
                     as what she once was ossified
              and was chiseled into a practice chanter
              for oblivion what could be more loved
                 than what was almost lived in
              gone marmoreal memorial *I'm yours*
                   and all the business *enjoy my body*
                 and all the unpleasant business
          of malediction parroted with a banality
                charming as charmed Ah me
                      to repeat *Ah me*
                as the business goes belly-up

I wanted to talk about the songs
of a dead folk singer who was friends
with my grandparents, a man who could
describe your sad sack story back to yourself
like Demodocus at the Mead Hall on Scherie.
I wanted to talk about perch and the imperiled
fisheries of Southeast Michigan, the restaurants
where the fishers sent their catches.
The phosphorous in the fields, blue-green algae in the harbor.
The reference to Lake Erie
I found while reading *Finnegan's Wake*
in Echo's Restaurant one January afternoon—
our lake lemanted, that greyt lack…
urban and orbal, though seep froms umber
under wasseres of Erie. The owner asked,
"Did it stop for a merciful moment, the ice storm?"
It had me thinking of the adjective "merciful" because I'm also scared
all the time of death and money,
of paucity and grift, by what might arrive in the mail
with the clap of tin, by excessive bilirubin
in the blood (can't be a liver and have a liver,
the ale taster in the night book says).
I'd watch the Lions at Echo's every Sunday
while reading a book and eating perch,
which sounds a lot like losing in Loserville
but the Lions have a way of getting you to pay
attention, which is to say they have unique
ways of losing, ways you haven't yet imagined.
They slow the awful sabbath down.
There's rarely such a chance to gaze languorously
inward and taste the afternoon like a morsel
(egg, flour, lemon, tartar sauce, the flesh of freshwater).

Yelping the Tegmine

It's a cluster in the constellation Cancer
and a crab shack near the Shell station on Telegraph Road.
The polysemy and the lump crab sandwiches are delicious.

The trains in these parts can hobble your commute, and if your inclination
is not to trust lump crab from a shot-and-beer roadhouse,
even a well-reviewed one, I don't blame you.

I recommend the sandwich though. It's flavorful and fresh,
and the area won't suffer for having hosted you.

They'll never buy into your epiphanies, so don't pretend to have them.
The moon is not a skiff with your inky spleen in its paren,
and the nearby park is not a closed paren within which
you might make a notation about Tycho Brahe's bare-eyed observations.

There is a sadness to bisque and beer, which is why I'm suggesting
the crab sandwich, the Zeta Cancri signature sandwich.

They'll never ask you to Yelp the place either. An old trucker friend
of mine lived upstairs after a bad break-up with his ex.

It's not much of a story: scotography, x-ray radiography,
a bunch of the boys were whooping it up, writing out the darkness.
The false ceiling, the dim lights, the wickerwork like bones.

It's a new year. It's the ecliptic of oil tankers
in the eyeline of that long glacial plain.
You must keep the big rigs' occultation in mind and search
unbidden Yelp reviews.
The afternoon's less dull for the thoughts of stars.

You don't have to sit here while you eat.
You can take the sandwich to the park and hiss back at the geese,
or do the geese honk? I believe it's both, and they also shit like dogs,
so maybe it's best to dine in and ask for a boilermaker.

Listen for whatever beered-up palaver echoes down the pine
and know there's a pleasant way of disappearing
in such a place without feeling quite alone.
If you sit upright in the stool, you can watch the bubbles

decamp for foam. It's a bird's-eye, not a god's-eye view
from above the ecliptic line the room can get on you.
The crab is not endemic to this place; it isn't what you'd call
"To die for," but as I've said elsewhere, it's very good.

"The Quinque Viae" and "The Myth of Sisyphus" as Non-Fungible Tokens

Tuned to the blood pressure cuff, the prick of the finger,
the transmissions from the dumb animal ripple
toward animalcules and what life is found in ditches,
the stethoscope inching down the back and over the sternum,
this set of words has sucked lemons and eructed crop milk
like a robin depositing in the beaks of young the bitter
sustenance that has kept me at it and will keep them.
That's my mother back there at St. Thomas Aquinas School
engaging in apologetics with Camus, whom she called a settler
for his attitudes about Algiers. Immutable leger—
I nearly said leisure—immutable leisure I take with me
to the window before the beach like wine, remembering
how paper thin I'd been just one winter ago, looking forward
to the season that was likely to precede the third season
in the deciduous forest region of the northern hemisphere
when the weather might give the crackling skin a break,
the globed areas of the brain on an imaging machine,
the first mover argument minted but still replicated
where the ways of the propulsive void must be discounted.

Yelping the Mr. Fresh Drive-Thru Convenience Store

Sunburnt against the vinyl tuck and roll
in a baseball card in spokes town, in
a steel mill town, fifteen axle bludgeoning
asphalt 'til it's buckled town, in an it all
must seem like trope automobile, I called
for a pack of Newports, a glass Coke bottle,
two oil cans of beer, a bag of Better Made,
a jar of aspirin, and margarine. He handed it off
through the sliding window with my change.
It was the driving through, the idling V-6,
the gerunds one could make of splendor
and torpor, the idyll of a summer I sort
of remember. The sun on the hood of the car...
I struggle to describe the sun, the hood
of the Impala Lake Erie green.
And another time later that year,
after the bar, in a snowstorm after the bar,
you melted the snow crystals on a brown paper bag
full of cold cuts and half-cartons of eggs
in your arms. A Red Wings broadcast
on the AM radio, a voice like snow
describing a brutal game on ice.
The heater core was failing and the windshield
rimed along a horizontal hairline crack.
Sometimes all the elements are there,
and there's nothing to say or want but
we loved each other then. Sometimes nothing
quite breaks and the dispassionate machinery
carries on. We called out for everything—
breath mints, milk, and bread—without
leaving the little world of that big car. I wish
I'd held onto that car (two two-by-fours

and rock salt in the trunk to keep
from getting stuck). I'm still toggling
between those seasons, placing them
in a year they never shared. That rear wheel
drive spinning us out and out until
we saw our house among the drifts.

Disambiguation With Chronotope and Vectors

Is there a day at your place
when what's unwanted and discarded
gets put out or, better yet,
an interminable series of days
that falls on the same day of the week
with the regularity of a hydraulic arm
hoisting a plastic barrel at seventy degrees?
Gwen, face crinkled from cigarettes
and vodka, you wonder more
about the Russian character in the novel
than the horse that pulls the plow
through the beanfield in boustrophedon.
Etiolated, wan Gwen, the pericope
you're working from is impossible,
yet there's a day when the bug-ridden
mattresses can be set out without
embarrassment, or at least without
a sense of shame. Is there a day, Gwen,
when what is loved pathologically
is abnegated in favor of new beginnings?
I'm thinking of cigarettes, eggs,
and coffee. I'm thinking of cedars
fanning dust over a concrete porch.
It might be a matter of edging them
to love them more. Breakfast might be
a matter of loving less to give them
edges. The text I was reading blurred
into a background of manila paper,
which for all I know might be how
you see things. I'm sure you can tell
how intent I am on the future. My future
intentions are pure as the turkey-footed

petioles that scatter in windstorms
and equally circumscribed by circumstance.
Will there be a day, Gwen, when acres
of scalloping newspapers will forsake
their hazard to your garage and adjacent
house, and even vectors will recalibrate
their routes? The big trucks belching smoke
will pause curbside and collect all
you've been too tired to relinquish
and the toilet paper wads in the broken
door handles will be replaced
with implements of polished brass
that will burnish in the palms of ghosts
that you once viewed as bitter.
There will come a day, Gwen,
when all of this is true.

Yelping the Waterfront

Bellied-up and whimpering about the eventuality
of being dead again at the Waterfront Restaurant
the evening of the Snow Moon which,
as you might imagine, is full and large, yet no larger
than its mass has been since before Tycho Brahe
eyeballed it against the backdrop of a strange star
in Cassiopeia, observing no parallax among the bodies
and concluding Aristotle's celestial immutability axiom
was wrong; it's a reflective gift the sun
brings itself to give us when it hits that plane.
I snap a picture above Ontario from across
the Trenton Channel. The river is a vitrine
displaying all the precious pieces of the sky.
It's the offseason of the boats that clog the strait,
of the leathered bodies that strafe themselves with sun.
The lights along the dock at the shuttered marina
spangle what can't sit still, spangle rivulets
in darkness, spangle reflections of the water
in tall windows (when landlocked I prefer
a half roundel looking into an indistinct,
unconstellated landscape) of an empty restaurant
whose grandeur could be missed from the potted stretch
of Jefferson one must drive to get here. Spangle
blue eyes, this wine glass, spangle because "coruscate"
sounds too strange and arcane, even for a poem
of mine, spangle the water from Ontario to here,
from here to Ontario—I think of Jake Dimmick,
bass player and friend, over there in Leamington
and wonder at the few short miles, the incommensurate
international boundary between us, the floating
mechanisms (ferries, jet skis, and cabin boats)
that draw on Archimedes' buoyancy principle

to take us toward and away from each other, the radio
check-ins with the Coast Guard, the white buoy
like a bomb casing that marks the border.
I think about the phone my wife dropped from a boat
in Lake Erie and wonder about its final ping
as I text her a picture of the moon above the water,
mathematical in its recurrence, inevitable
as what goes swimming in its light.

Grammar of the Birds

It's the late offseason of what
will never be. The RV park
by the inland sea is empty.
I clamber onto the exposed
poplar roots, their earth
gone to wind and surf,
to listen. A grist of calcium
sparkles in the sand.
The cooling towers
of the Fermi I and II reactors
exhale little puffs of steam
into the netted-mackerel sky
across the bay.
I've been hearing it since
before the dawn,
this finite automaton
syntax of the birds.
I've been a blind jag
between the branches,
a bigram in a phonological
bout, a memory house
made ridiculous
by repetition. These
two-birds-in-the-hand
truisms, this robin trill.
Without plumage,
I've been a hopeless birder
of disembodied song.
The Huron River Inn
at the mouth of the bay
is closed. There's a fishing boat
at the edge of the gravel lot,

some steelhead skeletons
combed over by the gulls.
Which is to say we become
what we cannot look
forward to, the way
a gastropod coils around
itself what is and is not
itself only to be plucked
through its aperture like light.

NOTES

The poem "Thought on Thought With Fried Chicken Getting Cold" quotes from and alludes to Eugene Field's poem "The Duel."

The poem "Dichotomy Paradox as a Non-Fungible Token" alludes to TS Eliot's "Little Gidding" and Ezra Pound's "The Seafarer." It also quotes briefly from Fanny Howe's poem "Between Delays."

"The Tuscan" referenced in "Canada, Approximately" is the astronomer Galileo.

The poem "The Starting Gate" alludes to the theme song from the TV show *Mr. Ed*.

The prose poem "Prologue to a Fiction" reprises a few lines from my poem "A Georgic for Sally and Darla," which appeared first in the journal *On the Seawall* and later in the book *Poolside at the Dearborn Inn*. The phrase, "whose fingers were the cradle of a lost and gentle logic," is an allusion to Terrance Hayes' brilliant book, *Hip Logic*. The poem ends with an allusion to Yeats' "When You Are Old."

In the poem "Tender Years: A Brief Memoir With *Eddie and the Cruisers*," the friend who says that "every poem is a persona poem" is the poet Stacy Gnall; she offered up this notion during her 2024 AWP presentation, "Nobody's Mother: Writing Through the Decision to Parent."

The poem "Yelping the Tegmine" quotes briefly from Robert Service's poem "The Shooting of Dan McGrew."

ACKNOWLEDGMENTS

I'd like to thank the editors of the following journals, magazines, and presses for first publishing these poems:

The Arkansas International: "Under the Tegmine"

Atticus Review: "Thought on Thought With Fried Chicken Getting Cold"

Bracken Magazine: "Words for Port Austin"

Belt Magazine: "Adrian Dantley (AD) Circa 1890s," "The City of Champions," "A Brief Survey of Regional Consumer Markets," and "Yelping the Huron River Inn"

Carolina Quarterly: "Disambiguation With Chronotope and Vectors" and "Racing Simulcast as Non-Fungible Token"

Clade Song: "Walleye Carcass as a Non-Fungible Token"

Diode: "Prologue to a Fiction" and "Yelping Ford Lanes"

EcoTheo Review: "Disambiguation With a Dead Carp on the Bank"

Eunoia Review: "The Weather of Our Names"

Exacting Clam: "Yelping Echo's"

Flyover Country: "Yelping the Bella Vista"

Grist: A Journal of the Literary Arts: "'The Quinque Viae' and 'The Myth of Sisyphus' as Non-Fungible Tokens"

J Journal: "Disambiguation With Fire Trucks at Elsinore"

Ligeia Magazine: "Yelping the Tegmine"

Menacing Hedge: "Must We on the Way to the Island"

One Art: "Starting Gate"

Oxford American: "Disambiguation With Coca-Cola, Helium, Carbon"

Open: A Journal of Arts & Letters: "Canada, Approximately" and "Disambiguation With Barry Sanders, Pluto, and Persephone"

Panoply: "Yelping the Mr. Fresh Drive-Thru Convenience Store"

Paperbark Literary Magazine: "Disambiguation With One Bird in the Hand"

Pøst: "Dichotomy Paradox as Non-Fungible Token"

Potomac Review: "Tender Years: a Brief Memoir With *Eddie and the Cruisers*"

Quarter After Eight: "Grammar of the Birds"

Roanoke Review: "Annotations While Waiting for the Mail and Thinking of My Mother"

Third Coast Magazine: "Those Vacation Plans You Made"

Westchester Review: "Tomorrow Fries An Egg"

The William and Mary Review: "Derecho"

Special thanks to Terrapin Books for first publishing "Epistle to the Donut Shop" in *The Book of Donuts* and to Finishing Line Press for publishing several of these poems in the chapbook *Yelping the Tegmine.*

* * *

I'd like to thank the following individuals: publisher Dr. Ross Tangedal, editor Brett Hill, cover designer Samantha Bjork, sales director Sophie McPherson, and the incredible team at Cornerstone Press; Dustin Pearson, Russell Thorburn, Kevin Cantwell, Zilka Joseph, Megan Schoen, Sherry Wynn Perdue, F. Daniel Rzicznek, Peter Markus, Ryan Dillaha, Catharine Batsios, Jassmine Parks, Reynaldo Hinojosa, M.L. Liebler, Shawntai Brown, Stacy Gnall, Nicholas Rombes, Stephen Pasqualina, Mary-Catherine Harrison, Amanda Laudig, David Hammontree, Robert Keast, Patrick O'Neill, Emily Choi, Mercedes Mejia, Glen Armstrong, Kelly Fordon, Alise Alousi, and Michael Lauchlan. Special thanks to Sarah Pazur, my everything, for her guidance and support.

CAL FREEMAN is the author of *Fight Songs* (2017) and *Poolside at the Dearborn Inn* (2022). His writing has appeared in many journals including *Atticus Review, Image, The Poetry Review, Verse Daily, Under a Warm Green Linden, North American Review, The Moth, Oxford American, River Styx, and Advanced Leisure.* He is a recipient of the Devine Poetry Fellowship (judged by Terrance Hayes), winner of *Passages North*'s Neutrino Prize, and a finalist for the River Styx International Poetry Prize. Born and raised in Detroit, he teaches at Oakland University and serves as Writer-In-Residence with InsideOut Literary Arts Detroit.